GALAXY EXPLORATIONS

Simple Techniques for Beginners

Megan John

Table of Contents

CHAPTER ONE

INTRODUCTION

Is it genuine that you need to sort out some way to draw a world night sky? In any case, could you say that you are worried about the likelihood that it will be excessively challenging for learners or that you are uncertain where to start? This illuminating activity will show you, every little push toward turn, how to paint a major universe night sky zero material cutoff points required. Accepting, to some degree for now, that you're searching for shockingly better night sky associations, look at this dazzling moon painting on dull material and this essential mermaid in moonlight painting. Which shades make up a structure? "What tones could it be smart for me to use in a world?" is the most significant inquiry you could make about yourself.

BIT BY BIT DIRECTION TO PAINT A CONSTRUCTION TIME SNEAK PAST

Bit by bit heading to Paint a Design with Trees (Smooth Way). Dull is the first assortment that calls an up close and personal response when you consider universes or space. However, large systems also contain a number of energetic buildup whirlwinds and gas known as fogs. Fogs come in red, red, blue, greenish blue, green, and white varieties.

Universe Painting Tones

1. Dull/Faint Blue

2. White

3. Red

4. Red

5. Blue

6. Green

7. White.

Get rolling into acrylic painting with this painting starter pack. Join underneath to thank your three companions: tips guide, a clever movement manual for the paint brush, and a printable rundown of provisions (with joins). I consent to receiving updates and messages. One of the most shocking ways of managing getting world contemplations is to see first class pictures from capable visual prepared experts. Considering a picture inspiration can help you with adding a few intriguing parts to your own thing of beauty. This could furthermore at any point help you with the shapes/degrees and even shades of your creation.

CHAPTER TWO

TIPS ON THE MOST FIT METHODOLOGY TO PAINT A WORLD NIGHT SKY WITH A WIPE

Survey that I was suggesting using an essential contraption to help with blending your universe.

It's a texture!

Using a wipe is unimaginably clear and an immeasurable contraption for fledglings. Wipes will help you with making bonehead affirmation and Astonishing blends missing a ton of effort. They are especially helpful for people who are just starting out and might find it difficult to mix paint in with a regular brush. I see that mixing paint in with a wipe is significantly less problematic and requires less expertise than utilizing a brush. Furthermore, it is engaging to utilize it.

KINDS OF WIPES FOR BLENDING

What kind of wipe works best?

It is possible to utilize this kind of skilled worker wipe, which I used in this educational activity. In any case, you can utilize a standard kitchen wipe for anything that period of time it is perfect to spend any more cash. In spite of the fact that they will create comparative outcomes, the talented specialist wipe will certainly have an all the more even appearance in general.

Ace Wipe

Preceding using the wipe, you'll use a 1 inch level brush to put your paint down. We won't mix in with a wipe in the going with stage, so you shouldn't worry about to be wonderful here or mix. Basically have a couple of extraordinary times and get as required with your paint on the material! The deals for the tones are (from outside edges, inside): at the base faint, blue, purple, pale pink, and light pink.

RULES TO MIX IN WITH A WIPE

Utilizing your preferred wipe, blend the limits between each tone. Move step by step up to the dullest beginning with the lightest. To blend in with a wipe go through a light and down spotting improvement like you're meandering. Do whatever it takes not to press absurdly hard or you'll crash paint from the material. This is the requirement for blending (to keep dull tones from obliterating the light tones).

1. Pink a light pink.

2. Pink with purple

3. Purple with blue

4. Dark blue with black

For each grouping mix, try to utilize a faultless piece of your wipe. Wash the wipe off with water when it no longer has clean regions. You can mix in with your brush in an equivalent requesting as above in the event that you don't have a wipe. With each mix, you can cause your brush to appear generally more appealing. Your smooth way gaudy structure sky's shape and shade are given by this first layer. Take a gander at the entire instructive development underneath until the end of the inventive creation steps.

TIPS OF BLENDING IN WITH A WIPE

1. Work with lightest game plans to generally diminish so you don't diminish the lightest mixes.

2. Mix by tenderly reaching your wipe (all over) along the line of groupings.

3. Utilize clean pieces of the wipe for each combination mix.

4. Wash the wipe when all regions are crusaded in paint.

THE BEST WAY TO PAINT STARS ON A FRAME

After you've finished painting the ground colors of your real-life night sky, you should add a few stars. It can be moved in a number of different ways. The essential technique is to splatter them, the second is to flick them with a toothbrush, and the third is to hand paint every one with just the right amount of round brush in the event that you need more command over where they go.

HOW COULD YOU FLICK PAINT FOR STARS?

Essential worries at the front, slight out your paint. How should acrylic paint be appropriated? Simply combine one tablespoon of water and a little white paint. It should have a thin fluid consistency, similar to skim milk. The following stage is to fundamentally plunge any brush I utilize a wide level brush in the diminished paint. From there on out, while holding the brush over your material, you'll start tapping it on another brush. To make splatter stars by and large around your material, you ought to move your brush around it. You will get additional remarkable stars from the previous few movies. As the paint leaves the fibers, the stars will turn out to be more modest as you tap your brush more. I had the choice to get all of the stars under with just a single dunk of my brush in the liquid paint. You can in like manner bring down an old toothbrush in the weakened paint for little stars to splatter. With your toothbrush ascended to bristle side down, use your thumb to flick the strands all over. You'll get little splatters of paint on your material. One thing I like to do following to using either the flick framework or the toothbrush methodology above, is to solidify extra stars with a sprinkle of round brush. This will allow you more control and remember stars for your sky where it's more uncovered.

There are central stages for how to paint a universe on a material with acrylic paints. While making a pass at something new I customarily really like in any case genuinely 5"x 7" material and move reliably up to bigger parts later on. In most cases, it is entirely up to you to decide what is acceptable. Simply ensure that the material of any size you choose does not frighten or compromise you. It is basic to allow yourself to commit mistakes while working on any of your most important beginner craftsmanship projects. Essentially attempt to have a material and a few paints to work with. I use Liquitex Huge Acrylic paints yet any critical bodied paint will truly endorse. You'll besides require a few devices to accomplish our ideal limitless impacts. There are two key instruments, truly.

1.   A wipe. Specialist and ordinary sea wipes, too as customary family wipes, can be used. Painters' wipes, like the ones in the image, are what I suggest.

2.   a toothpaste. This seems like the easiest method for getting a lot of stars. Some will prepare you to use one of your paint brushes for this, yet I've forever been not able to get that to honorably work. Most of the work and required results can be accomplished with these two devices alone. The wipe is for the gas clouds while the toothbrush is for our stars. You are as of now ready to begin since you have gathered your leaned toward size of

material, wipes, paints, and toothbrush. The ongoing second, you may be considering what colors you ought to make a framework painting. The cool thing about painting grandiose designs is you can do essentially anything you want. It's easy to paint on, and any mistakes can be fixed quickly. Like how liberal hypothetical masterpieces are! Which by the way are another remarkable painting project for youngsters to endeavor. I eagerly propose assessing some speculative craftsmanship projects when you get depleted being the master of frameworks. In addition to the other way around, your capacity to create worlds may benefit your theoretical practices. Something new that will assist you with making your universes is zeroing in on different pictures of genuine universes that we have. Your visual library will have the data you want to make your own tolerant you contribute some energy seeing at authentic pictures of guaranteed vainglorious systems as well as those that others have painted. You can likewise find out about a portion of the decisions you could have to make thanks to this. A self important starburst system known as more turbulent 82 is depicted here. In the social event of stars known as Urea Major, it is twelve million light years away. There are layers of light blue, red, white, and perhaps purple, as may be undeniable. A cool perspective in regards to painting and drawing is you habitually will wind up getting impelled by the subject past what you could have been quite a bit early. You out of nowhere begin investigating little subtleties. Recall two or three fundamental principles of development, similar to the norm of thirds, while starting your masterpiece. I excuse that sporadically. To the extent that creation, the way things are depicted is essentially better compared to anything I ended up doing. Exactly when we get to the methods that are underneath, you will have a predominant cognizance of what I mean. Here is just one more portrayal of how you can in a general sense go with anything colors you really care about. As you can see, there are different decisions concerning the blend bed you should work with. This one is a mix of blue and green.

Red, blue, and purple are phenomenal varieties to join. You can go monochromatic and use basically shades of blue or shades purple. You can go with an extra like tones like light blue, blue and purple. You clearly moreover need essentially isolating was well for your experience and stars. This is a wonderful juvenile painting dare to help with starting discernment you could unwind blending and mixing of assortments. It could similarly lay the reason for coming about associations. Assisting one in comprehending the various methods for creating a stunning night sky, such as for a painting of a night scene.

For my motivations, I'm just a geek that couldn't need anything over to eventually have the choice to make signs of room faring redesigns. In a little while, I stay mindful of that you ought to exploit your phenomenal creative powers and use the going with advances toward make your very own universe.

CHAPTER THREE

BASIC ERRANDS FOR HOW TO PAINT A FRAMEWORK

Resulting to doing a portion of these syntheses these methods are truly easy to follow and will get you from basic human status up to magnificent powers of signs.

STEP 1: You ought to begin with only a dark material. You can simply apply a layer of dark paint or purchase dark materials. Permit it to dry and forge ahead toward the accompanying stage.

STEP 2: Then, at that point, you need to use your wipe to apply your most dark assortments first. Additionally, you could apply the paint with a brush and then wipe it off with your wipe. You want to have a couple of districts significant with the faint assortment and a while later develop out to get the gas like effect of a cloud world. You can add on an incredible arrangement immediately or a little at a time. It is totally subject to you. Take the necessary steps not to fear committing blunders. You can always cover them up.

STEP 3: You ought to then add your mid tones. While working your lighter tones on to the material you should consider where your stars will go. Think about how that light releases from those spots and how it obscures as it moves further away.

STEP 4: Then you want to add your most splendid tones. You will start to see that your material is starting to obtain this gassy impact as you add each layer. You could attempt to begin to imagine what sort of creatures could exist in this world. Permit your mind to wander and share at the same time.

STEP 5: By and by you want to set up that toothbrush. We will incorporate our stars. To accomplish this, you will need a small cup or holder in which to apply some white paint. The paint ought to then be diminished with a touch of water. Not an exorbitant measure of yet with the eventual result of loosening up it. Then, take your toothbrush and risk the tip into your mix. Make sure to let any paint that's too much drip off. You can in like manner flick some off into your holder. By and by when you go to apply your stars you should get your toothbrush extremely close to the locale of the material where you want your central gatherings. The most awe inspiring bits of your masterpiece are where the most and most prominent stars should be. At the point when you get your packs in you can pull the range back further from the material to get a greater flow of stars.

STEP 6: Then, at that point, you really want to continue to add several extra layers of assortments with your wipe. In most cases, I will use a little darkness to cover up some of the material in areas where I need more dark space. I don't completely cover the stars because when the dark paint dries, it separates from them and makes them appear to be further away. I similarly will by and large turn out a part of the concealed districts as well. This helps add significance to your universe. As you can see from the progression of pictures the point of convergence of this starburst world changed imperceptibly from stage 5 to organize 6. I added somewhat more blue since I thought the red streak was somewhat areas of strength for excessively awkward.

STEP 7: Finally, add a couple of greater stars with your paintbrush in locale of your reality that are more splendid and consequently should have a greater more observable star. You can put these any spot you want, honestly. The real reason for Stage 7 is to finish your world. Tidy up the gas influences a piece where required. Dark up anything required as well. If you feel like the test, you can add a few planets, space rocks, or even a spaceship here! Here is the essential painting I did where I added planets. For crafted by craftsmanship I did in the model, I felt like the Starburst Universe itself was adequate. I wrongly focused it to a limit and dismissed the norm of thirds. At a time like the one depicted in the first image, it would have been exceptional. Taking everything into account, this is essentially all that to painting vast frameworks. There is clearly considerably more we could get into concerning painting a vast framework anyway this is the simplest method for managing it.

FIGURING OUT HOW TO PAINT PLANETS

At last I will figure out more and I will foster this later to consolidate space tests, spaceships, and space lodgings. Foregrounds could also be done in the future. Perhaps a scene under a night sky, There are great deals of layout style materials where a splendid night establishment will be significant to know how to make. Comparatively in like manner with another subject or part we put into our craftsmanship's, there are various approaches to developing this foundation. It is basically an issue of carving out a time to develop top of this. Developing a psychological visual library is the way to turning into an extraordinary craftsman. We should simply have some good times learning the essentials and painting a few cool universes on material for the present. Do whatever it takes not to be uncertain.

CHAPTER FOUR

STEP BY STEP INSTRUCTIONS TO PAINT A STAR-FILLED

Universe is an expertise with so many various techniques that you can paint exactly the same thing in 1,000,000 unique ways. A couple of pictures are more equipped for specific kinds of methodologies, yet others are at their best when it seems like testing. I needed to truly figure out how to embrace that with an instructional exercise because everyone makes decisions in unexpected ways. I need to tell you the best way to paint a system in this article, yet I won't offer you every one of the responses. My real goal is to help you create a system that is unique to you by focusing on making sense of more than just telling. We overall methodology these things surprisingly, which is the explanation I keep up with that this ought to be all the more an assistant as opposed to anything.

WHAT TO RECOLLECT FOR YOUR STAR-FILLED WORLD

The key thing that you need to address when it comes time to paint a framework kinds of parts you want to recall for your image. Every universe is thoroughly intriguing, outlined across reality from many materials. The end result of this is a mix of different parts in a large number of spots. You can single out what it feels ideal for you, but there are several fundamental parts in a framework that you probably need to have. The huge differentiation between the faint void of room and a great framework is in it, and what that resembles.

THE MOST IMPORTANT PHASE IN PAINTING A STAR-OCCUPIED UNIVERSE

The basic space is the principal thing you totally should remember for your cosmic system. Every framework has a great many splendid and shining things making stunning shapes, yet these wouldn't exist using any and all means without the incorporating space. To that end you ought to consistently recall the certified dead void of space for your image to make different parts pop. Unwind, this is shockingly fun.

THE SECOND PUSH TOWARD PAINTING A STAR-FILLED INESTIMABLE FRAMEWORK

The second thing that you ought to need to make a stunning star-filled infinite framework is undeniable: stars. Make universes so stunning stars. While various parts are cool, stars carry an everyday presence that is all their own. Remember the stars in the night sky; I presently can't seem to meet anybody who wasn't absolutely enchanted by them. Guarantee that you add a great deal of stars in all shapes and sizes to make an image that genuinely draws in your group. Exactly when you sort out some way to paint a framework, you ought to sort out some way to paint one critical part: planets. Basically every world has planets in all shapes and sizes filling the locale. Since Pluto was downsized, we have all discussing is a planet, however you control your world. This infers that you can make your planets as enormous, little, or wild as the need might arise. The critical part is that you make heads or tails of the workmanship piece for yourself and move starting there. When you add planets, you can really be creative. Anyway those are the three fundamental pieces of a universe; there is for the most part space for more if you really need to. Right when you sort out some way to paint a universe, you can add meteors, moon buildup, and falling stars whatever amount of it fulfills you.

My #1 thing about painting a framework is that generally the more creative you are, the better it look through over the long haul. Have a few great times here picking and adding more humble parts to give your material greater significance, truly.

THE BEST STRATEGY TO PAINT THE SPACE PART OF YOUR REALITY

For by far most, room itself either stimulates them or alerts them. This is because of how big it is and how mysterious it is. Like how vast water in the sea can appear to be a little overpowering, a great many people are careful about it. While you can undeniably utilize this with respect to picking how to paint an inestimable framework, you ought to warm it up. All things considered, my main thing about a fair world structure is the assortments, which is the explanation I like to utilize them whatever amount of I can, whether or not it has all the earmarks of being straightforward. The most common way of painting the space foundation regularly starts with a genuinely clear establishment. The most distorted space establishment that you can paint is to cover the material absolutely in dim. For specific people, this is all that they like to do, and that is absolutely alright. On occasion using an unmistakable establishment can genuinely help with making various parts of your reality hang out in an extraordinary way. Finish up what feels right to you and work starting there. My assumption is that you can use this manual for return and endeavor to make different styles of universes and see their thought process about. If dim feels exorbitantly incredible for you, you can persistently assess a dull blue in light of everything and check whether that feels more tone legitimate.

CHAPTER FIVE

APPROACHES TO ADDING GREATER SIGNIFICANCE

If you could manage without to look at the demanding depleted of space, which is absolutely okay too. There are numerous unusual methods for enhancing a plain delete foundation. By far most choose to use integrate various assortments like blues and purples to give their space a more neighborly look with barely sufficient greater significance. It can take your view from a science fiction thrill ride over to a more upbeat and more marvelous domain worth exploring. Painting a system requires more than simply painting a dark foundation with a few stars. You really want to make it individual, so take out the whole of your different blues and purples and see how you can use them to illuminate your sky. Right when you find the assortments that you use, be prepared to be a piece finished with your material. In spite of the fact that you are allowed to be essentially as amazing as you like with the foundation of your work of art, you ought to try not to be excessively awesome. I just partake in the natural nature of numerous cosmic systems. Utilize the blue and purple to make vague shapes that look natural. Instead of a specific square or circle, let the edges of your shapes obscure into one another or blend them out of spotlight. This helps you achieve a novel appearance similar to gleaming in space. These gleaming pops of variety can be made anywhere, but I think they are most impressive near the piece's center. I like this look since it draws in the look right to the center where your best vast framework parts will be.

BIT BY BIT GUIDELINES TO PAINT PLANETS

Sorting out some way to paint a world strategy adding your planets after you have finished the sky landscape. Painting planets is a clear cycle, yet it leaves the most space for ingenuity. Planets will frequently be a singular circle either left alone or with including parts. To make them greater or more modest, you can add shakes, moons, or rings to the area. Try to be creative when you get the chance to work on these. Use different assortments, play with plans, and perceive how you could make the image more enthusiastic. You can keep the same colors or give each planet its own distinct look. Here, I truly appreciate exploring different avenues regarding different varieties and examples to see what impact they have on the picture. It's is an extraordinary opportunity to illuminate your image for specific horseplay tones, indeed.

INSTRUCTIONS TO PAINT STARS

Painting stars is a fundamental piece of figuring out how to paint a universe, yet these are not your common stars. We all in all sorted out some way to draw a clear star as children, yet stars in show-stoppers will commonly be less portrayed. Tracking down the most ideal way to catch the shine of a star is more troublesome than characterizing its rakish edges on the grounds that a star is actually just sparkle. There are perhaps a couple of ways to deal with this, and I most definitely see that the best method for doing this is to mix an extensive variety of star styles to make a more convoluted picture. Again, sorting out some way to paint a universe is a singular effort, so work with what feels right to you. I understand what I like, yet that won't generally be the most effective way to get things done. That is the greatness of workmanship. With respect to painting a framework, you want to find the right tones. By far most will paint stars in a wonderful way that consolidates different whites and yellows. Varying shades can add such a ton of significance to your structure by and large, which is the explanation I for the most part ask people to use various shades. It adds an unpredictability that universes have, in reality. In this manner, before you begin sprinkling stars to consume the spaces between planets, pick your assortment plot.

THE MOST CLEAR TECHNIQUE FOR PAINTING A STAR

The most direct technique for painting a star is to use a fundamental spot. One of the most outstanding ways of making a key star in your world is to make a minuscule sphere, which I love for various reasons. Notwithstanding the way that it is basic enough for anyone to do, yet it is in like manner ideal for consuming in the spaces between various parts. If anything feels unnecessarily open or clear, add a lot of little circles to restore a vacant space. A really basic trick can change masterpieces an incredible arrangement. It isn't the most beautiful piece of sorting out some way to paint an enormous framework, yet it is strong, and I love it for that. You may be more acquainted with the accompanying sort of star. By painting four focuses up, down, left, and right, you can make a direct star shape. I trust that moving the parts of these centers is an effective philosophy, but I truly have my top options. I want to expand the top and base focuses more. This is a great way to add something special and wonderful to this look, especially because it looks like its sparkling. The last kind of star is an all around blend of the others. You will accept ought to begin with a circle and a while later extend light emanations out from it subtly. Do whatever it takes not to make them unnecessarily extended and endeavor to make them shift long. This makes it easier to really see the stars' beautiful glow and gives you more room to give them personality. The veritable heavenliness of a universe is the sparkle that we in general love to look at. Worlds are famous because they are extraordinary structures in space that frequently shine absolutely brilliantly. Adding a nice shimmer to your reality after various parts are completely managed fundamentally infers taking more splendid assortments like yellows, blues, and purples, and adding a shade around a piece of your parts. You will value how much this fills your enormous framework with a fascinating and extraordinary impression of life.

END

Right when you know how to paint a framework, it is something that you probably will not want to stop doing. It might be a helpful scene to paint, and since you can consistently change everything around, there is another thing to make. You'll notice that I didn't specify which tools to use with this because I have to give it to you. Put away an edge to assess different instruments and see what feels right. Wipes, brushes, and sharp edges can be verifiably helpful here, but everything spins around what feels fitting for you.

THE END

www.ingramcontent.com/pod-product-compliance
Lightning Source LLC
Chambersburg PA
CBHW071216290526
45796CB00008B/268